SPORTS ALL-STARS

TOM BRADY

Eric Braun

Lerner Publications ◆ Minneapolis

Lerner Publications Company
A division of Lerner Publishing Group, Inc.
241 First Avenue North
Minneapolis, MN 55401 USA

For reading levels and more information, look up this title at www.lernerbooks.com.

Main body text set in Albany Std 15/22. Typeface provided by Agfa.

Library of Congress Cataloging-in-Publication Data

Names: Braun, Eric, 1971–
Title: Tom Brady / Eric Braun.
Description: Minneapolis : Lerner Publications, [2016] | Series: Sports All-Stars | Includes bibliographical references and index. | Audience: Ages: 7–11. | Audience: Grades: 4 to 6.
Identifiers: LCCN 2016018152 (print) | LCCN 2016020246 (ebook) | ISBN 9781512425796 (lb : alk. paper) | ISBN 9781512431247 (pb : alk. paper) | ISBN 9781512428308 (eb pdf)
Subjects: LCSH: Brady, Tom, 1977——Juvenile literature. | Football players—United States—Biography—Juvenile literature. | Quarterbacks (Football)—United States—Biography—Juvenile literature.
Classification: LCC GV939.B685 B73 2016 (print) | LCC GV939.B685 (ebook) | DDC 796.332092 [B] —dc23

LC record available at https://lccn.loc.gov/2016018152

Manufactured in the United States of America
1-41347-23291-7/27/2016

CONTENTS

QUARTERBACK GREAT

Tom Brady throws a pass during Super Bowl XLIX.

Calm and in control.

That's how Tom Brady felt in the fourth quarter of Super Bowl XLIX on February 1, 2015. His New England Patriots were down by 10 points. They had jumped out to an early lead, outplaying the Seattle Seahawks. But fans called Seattle's fierce defense the Legion of Boom for a reason. They tackled Brady for a **sack** and snagged two **interceptions**. Then the Seahawks' offense got hot. Quarterback Russell Wilson led the team to 17 points. Going into the final period, Seattle was up, 24–14.

Did Brady panic? Not a chance. Instead, he did what he does best.

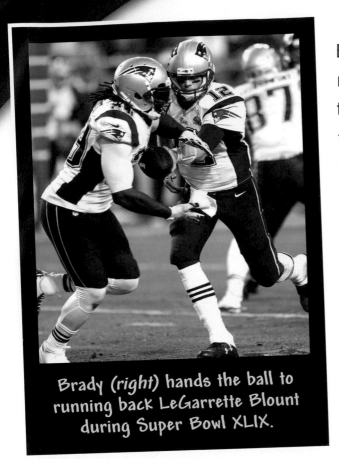

Brady (right) hands the ball to running back LeGarrette Blount during Super Bowl XLIX.

Brady took control and rallied his team. Over the next few minutes, the Patriots drove for two touchdowns. Brady hit wide receiver Julian Edelman for the second touchdown with about two minutes left in the game. Just like that, New England had the lead, 28–24. Brady had set up his team for victory again.

The Seahawks still had a chance. They drove down the field. With one yard to go for a touchdown, Wilson threw a pass. Patriots **rookie** Malcolm Butler grabbed the ball for an interception. The win was sealed for New England!

The Patriots erupted in cheers. For Brady, this was Super Bowl victory number four. Many fans would remember the game for Seattle's decision on the one-yard line. Why would they pass instead of run with only one yard to gain? But if Brady hadn't led his team's comeback, Seattle's blunder would not have mattered.

Many quarterbacks put up big numbers. Tom Brady's heroics in the biggest games set him apart from the rest. Year after year, he delivers at the most important times. He is nearing 40 years old—a time when most football players have long since retired. Yet Brady is still playing at a peak level. He may not be finished collecting Super Bowl trophies.

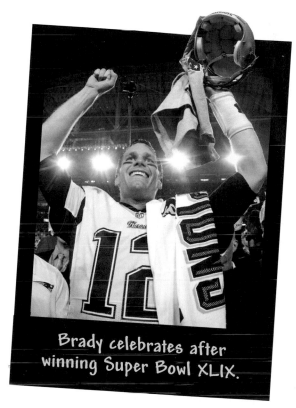

Brady celebrates after winning Super Bowl XLIX.

Around the world, more than 114 million people watched Super Bowl XLIX on TV. That made it the most watched TV show ever at the time.

STUDENT OF THE GAME

Brady during his years at the University of Michigan

During Tom Brady's years at the University of Michigan, a star quarterback was always on the football team. The problem was, it wasn't Brady. First, there was Brian Griese. He led the

Players soak Lloyd Carr as the Wolverines celebrate a win in 1999.

Michigan Wolverines to the 1997 national title. Then there was Drew Henson. Michigan coach Lloyd Carr said Henson was "the most talented quarterback that I've been around."

In 1998, Brady was in his fourth year at Michigan. He was forced to compete for the starting job with Henson, a freshman. His coach preferred the younger, more talented player. So did the fans. Nobody saw Brady as a star. He was average: average arm, average body, average talent.

Brady worked to get better. He watched videos of football games almost every night. He studied defenses. He learned how other teams played. He worked on his throwing accuracy. He learned to spot open receivers *before* they got open. And he began to develop the skill that would help him so much in the future: the ability to stay calm under pressure.

Coach Carr had Brady share time on the field with Henson. But the coach soon noticed the older player's **poise** and improved play. Finally, halfway through the 1999 season, Brady became the starting quarterback. It was his fifth year at the school.

In 1999, Brady threw 16 touchdown passes in 11 games for Michigan.

Football fans caught a glimpse of what a great quarterback Brady could be in a game against Penn State. The day began poorly for him. He threw three interceptions and was sacked six times. The Wolverines were down by 10 points in the fourth quarter. But with an aching body and a bloody face, Brady led his team to the win, 31–27. Several weeks later, he finished his college career with a win over Alabama in the Orange Bowl.

Even after proving himself at Michigan, Brady was not seen as a great player by football **scouts**. He was taken in the sixth round of the 2000 NFL draft by the New England Patriots—the 199th player chosen. With the Patriots, he again found himself stuck behind a quarterback the head coach thought was more athletic.

Michigan has won the college football national championship 11 times. The first time was in 1901. The most recent championship was in 1997.

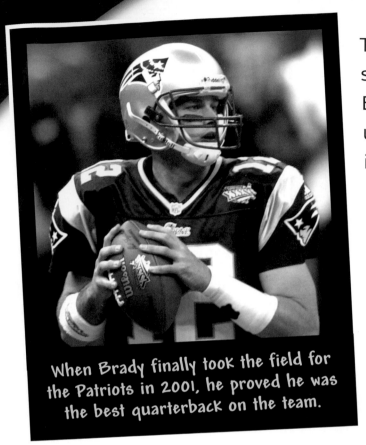

When Brady finally took the field for the Patriots in 2001, he proved he was the best quarterback on the team.

This time the starter was Drew Bledsoe. It wasn't until Bledsoe was injured in 2001 that Brady got to start. Brady then led the Patriots to a Super Bowl victory—his first of many.

If Brady hadn't faced doubts along the way—from Michigan fans and even from his own coach—he might not have worked so hard. He might not have learned to prepare so well. Without being forced to prove himself, he might have remained average.

Football isn't the only sport that Brady enjoys.

Do you have a busy schedule? School, homework, soccer practice, guitar lessons . . . Sure, that's pretty busy. But it's not *Tom Brady* busy. Tom Brady's days are scheduled down to the minute.

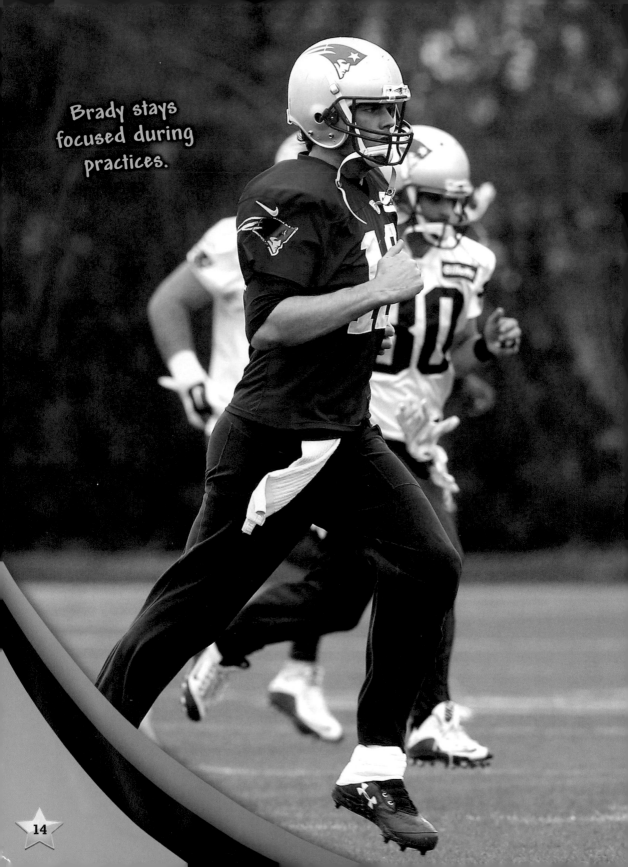

Brady stays focused during practices.

Every detail, every single day. His workouts. His meetings. His games and practices. His sleep. His meals. Even his vacations. Brady sets some workout schedules *years* in advance.

Every NFL player works hard. Success at the highest level takes a lot of effort. But after 15 years in the NFL, Brady is playing as well as he ever has—maybe better.

Brady's schedule keeps him moving, but he often takes time to talk with fans.

Part of the reason is his diet. Every meal is carefully planned to be healthful. When he wants to celebrate a big win with a special treat, he has ice cream—ice cream made of vegetables, that is.

Brady also takes care of his body with exercise. He uses **resistance bands** instead of heavy weights.

Brady runs at the beach as part of his training.

This helps keep his muscles flexible as well as strong. Brady works out at the gym, on the soft sand at the beach, and in the water. The soft sand and water help prevent injuries.

Probably the most important exercises Brady does are for his mind. He does brain exercises to calm his mind at night. That helps him fall asleep early and wake up on time without an alarm. He trains his brain to help him think quickly. On the field, this comes in handy when Brady has just seconds to react. He does brain drills that help his vision and memory too.

"The body is a whole system," Brady said. "That includes the brain. I feel like that's really where my edge is."

Brady may not have a free minute to look forward to until he retires. But that's OK with the star quarterback. If he has his way, he might not retire until he's 50.

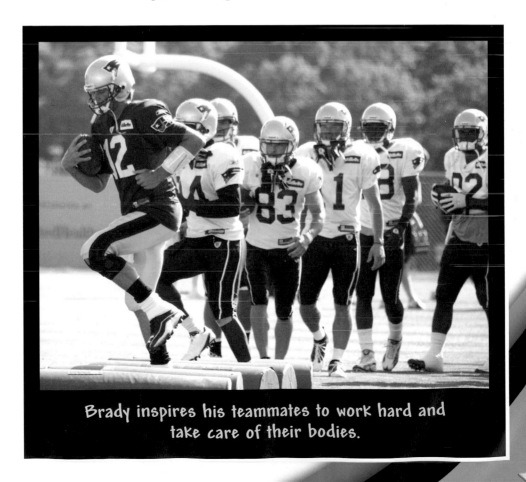

Brady inspires his teammates to work hard and take care of their bodies.

Brady and his wife, Gisele Bundchen, in 2011

This photo of Brady and his son, Benjamin, was taken at a park in 2014.

On the football field, Tom Brady is a volcano. He's full of fire that might erupt at any time. He screams at referees who may have missed a call. He gets in the face of his teammates if they blow a play. He goes toe-to-toe with the other team's **linebackers**.

Brady has three children: sons Jack (*front*) and Benjamin (*back*), and daughter Vivian (*not pictured*).

Off the field, Brady is much quieter. He keeps his personal life private as much as he can. When you're a celebrity, that can be tough. When you're married to an even bigger celebrity, that can be *really* tough. Brady's wife is supermodel Gisele Bundchen. For Brady and Bundchen, even going to the playground with their kids can make the news.

In early 2015, Brady's privacy took a hit. He was accused of having footballs deflated so he could grip them better. This is against NFL rules. The league investigated, and Brady's e-mails were made public. It was upsetting for the quarterback.

In one of the e-mails, Brady talked about his friend and rival, Peyton Manning. Brady is often compared to Manning, another superstar quarterback. Manning played for the Indianapolis Colts and the Denver Broncos. The two are about the same age. But in the e-mail, Brady stated that he had many seasons left in the NFL, while Manning probably had one or two.

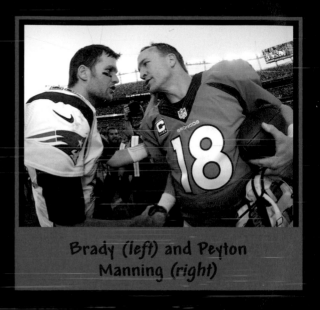

Brady (left) and Peyton Manning (right)

Brady defeated Manning 11 of the 17 times they met on the football field. But Manning won 3 of 5 **postseason** matchups. Brady holds the edge in total playoff and Super Bowl wins.

Brady apologized to Manning for the embarrassing e-mail. But part of it has already come to pass. Manning retired after winning the 2016 Super Bowl, less than two years after Brady's e-mail.

Brady (left) wears UGG boots on his way to a photo shoot for the footwear company.

If you ever get to visit Tom Brady at his home, you'll notice many pairs of UGG slippers near the entrance. Visitors are asked to take off their shoes and choose a pair of slippers to wear in the house. Brady is a **spokesperson** for the footwear company. A recent UGG advertising campaign focused on the joy of "doing nothing." That's a funny idea when you think about Brady's busy schedule.

In between his job and family time, Brady does a lot of work for charities. He's especially known for his work with Best Buddies International. The group works to help those with Down syndrome, autism, and other developmental conditions.

Brady has fun with his friends at Best Buddies International.

POSTSEASON POWERHOUSE

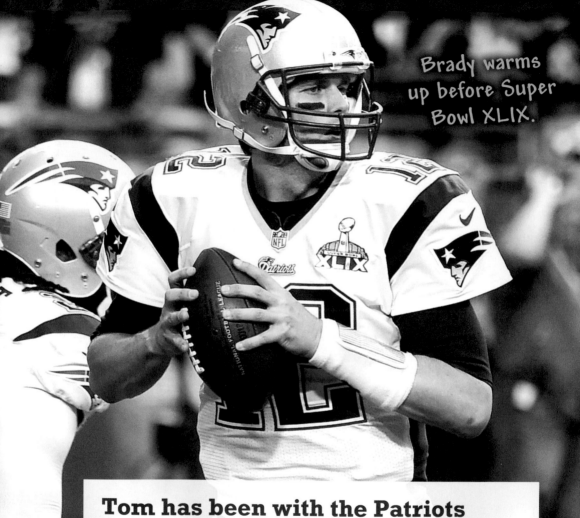

Brady warms up before Super Bowl XLIX.

Tom has been with the Patriots since 2000. During that time, no team in the NFL has enjoyed more success. The 2015 season was no different. The team won 10 games before their first loss. Then, in their first playoff game, they beat the Kansas City Chiefs.

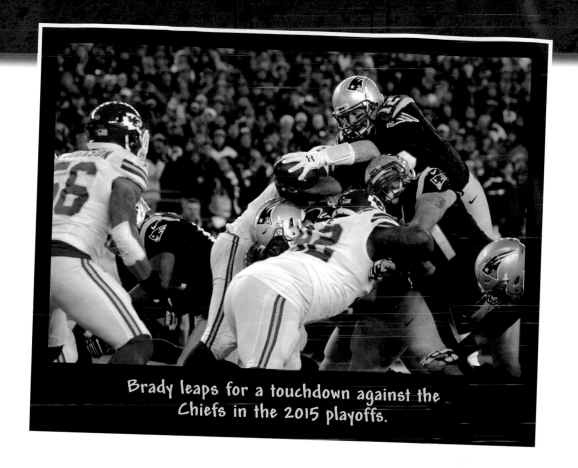
Brady leaps for a touchdown against the Chiefs in the 2015 playoffs.

But they couldn't get past Peyton Manning and the Broncos. Denver went on to win Super Bowl 50.

In 2015, Tom Brady had one of his best years yet. He completed 402 passes, the most of his career. He totaled 4,770 yards and 36 touchdowns. In the playoff win over the Chiefs, Brady tossed two touchdown passes. He also ran the ball into the end zone himself for another touchdown.

The Lombardi Trophy is given to the team that wins the Super Bowl. Brady has won the trophy four times.

By most measures, Brady is the greatest postseason quarterback of all time. In the playoffs, he has completed 738 passes for 7,957 yards. Both marks are all-time records. He has thrown 56 touchdowns in the postseason, which is also the most ever. As you might expect, Brady also holds the record for most postseason wins by a quarterback (22).

The Patriots missed Super Bowl 50, but Brady has been to the big game a record *six* times. He has won four Super Bowls and been named MVP in three of them. Brady has agreed to play for the Patriots through the 2019 season, when he'll be 42 years old. Given how well he is still playing, there's a good chance he'll add to those totals.

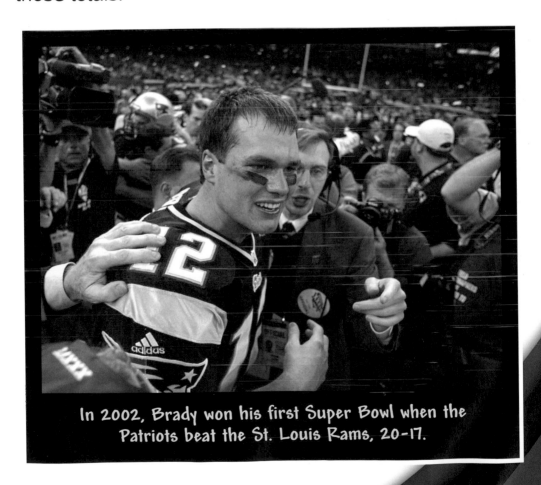

In 2002, Brady won his first Super Bowl when the Patriots beat the St. Louis Rams, 20-17.

All-Star Stats

There's little doubt that Tom Brady is the greatest postseason quarterback of all time. The statistics are clear. But what about the biggest game of all, the Super Bowl? The numbers speak loudly here too.

Most Career Super Bowl Pass Completions

164 Tom Brady, New England Patriots (6 games)
103 Peyton Manning, Indianapolis Colts/Denver Broncos (4 games)
83 Joe Montana, San Francisco 49ers (4 games)
83 Kurt Warner, St. Louis Rams/Arizona Cardinals (3 games)
81 Jim Kelly, Buffalo Bills (4 games)

Most Career Super Bowl Passing Yards

1,605 Tom Brady, New England Patriots (6 games)
1,156 Kurt Warner, St. Louis Rams/Arizona Cardinals (3 games)
1,142 Joe Montana, San Francisco 49ers (4 games)
1,128 John Elway, Denver Broncos (5 games)
1,001 Peyton Manning, Indianapolis Colts/Denver Broncos (4 games)

Most Career Super Bowl Touchdown Passes

13 Tom Brady, New England Patriots (6 games)
11 Joe Montana, San Francisco 49ers (4 games)
9 Terry Bradshaw, Pittsburgh Steelers (4 games)
8 Roger Staubach, Dallas Cowboys (4 games)
6 Kurt Warner, St. Louis Rams/Arizona Cardinals (3 games)
6 Steve Young, San Francisco 49ers (2 games)

Source Notes

9 Michael Rosenberg, "Tom Brady as You Forgot Him," *Sports Illustrated,* January 9, 2012, http://www.si.com/vault/2012/01/09/106148035/tom-brady-as-you-forgot-him.

17 Greg Bishop, "Given the Way He Prepares, Tom Brady Won't Be Slowing Down Anytime Soon," *Sports Illustrated*, December 10, 2014, http://www.si.com/nfl/2014/12/10/tom-brady-new-england-patriots-age-fitness?page=4&devicetype=default.

22 Barrett Wertz, "Tom Brady Does Nothing," *Men's Fitness,* accessed May 27, 2016, http://www.mensfitness.com/styleandgrooming/fashion/tom-brady-does-nothing.

Glossary

interception: when a pass is caught by the defending team

linebacker: a defender who usually plays in the middle of the field

poise: self-confidence, or an ability not to get upset in stressful situations

postseason: games played after the regular season to decide a champion

resistance band: an exercise band usually made of strong, thin rubber with handles on the ends

rookie: a first-year player

sack: when the quarterback is tackled for a loss of yards before he is able to throw the ball

scout: a person who judges the abilities and talent of football players

spokesperson: someone who appears in advertisements and makes statements on behalf of a company

Further Information

Braun, Eric. *Super Football Infographics*. Minneapolis: Lerner Publications, 2015.

Fishman, Jon M. *Russell Wilson*. Minneapolis: Lerner Publications, 2015.

New England Patriots
http://www.patriots.com

Savage, Jeff. *Tom Brady*. Minneapolis: Lerner Publications, 2015.

Sports Illustrated Kids. *Big Book of Who: Football*. New York: Time Home Entertainment, 2015.

Sports Illustrated Kids: Football
http://www.sikids.com/football

Index

Photo Acknowledgments

The images in this book are used with the permission of: © iStockphoto.com/iconeer
(gold and silver stars); © Jim McIsaac/Getty Images, p. 2; AP Photo/Ben Liebenberg,
pp. 4, 5, 6; AP Photo/Ric Tapia, p. 7; AP Photo/Scott Audette, p. 8; AP Photo/J. Pat
Carter, p. 9; © Rick Stewart/Getty Images, p. 10; AP Photo/Steven Senne, p. 12;
© Stickman/Bauer-Griffin/GC Images/Getty Images, p. 13; © Elsa/Getty Images,
p. 14; © Jessey Dearing for The Boston Globe/Getty Images, p. 15; © GONZALO/
Bauer-Griffin/GC Images/Getty Images, p. 16; © Damian Strohmeyer /Sports
Illustrated/Getty Images/Getty Images, p. 17; © Dimitrios Kambouris/FilmMagic/Getty
Images, p. 18; © Stickman/Bauer-Griffin/GC Images/Getty Images, p. 19; © Paul
Hiffmeyer/Disneyland Resort/Getty Images, p. 20; AP Photo/David Drapkin, p. 21;
© Stickman/Bauer-Griffin/GC Images/Getty Images, p. 22; © On Sport/Getty Images,
p. 24; © Barry Chin/The Boston Globe/Getty Images, p. 25; AP Photo/Winslow
Townson, p. 26; © Sporting News/Getty Images, p. 27.

Front cover: © Jim McIsaac/Getty Images (Tom Brady); © iStockphoto.com/
neyro2008 (motion lines); © iStockphoto.com/ulimi (black and white stars);
© iStockphoto.com/iconeer (gold and silver stars).